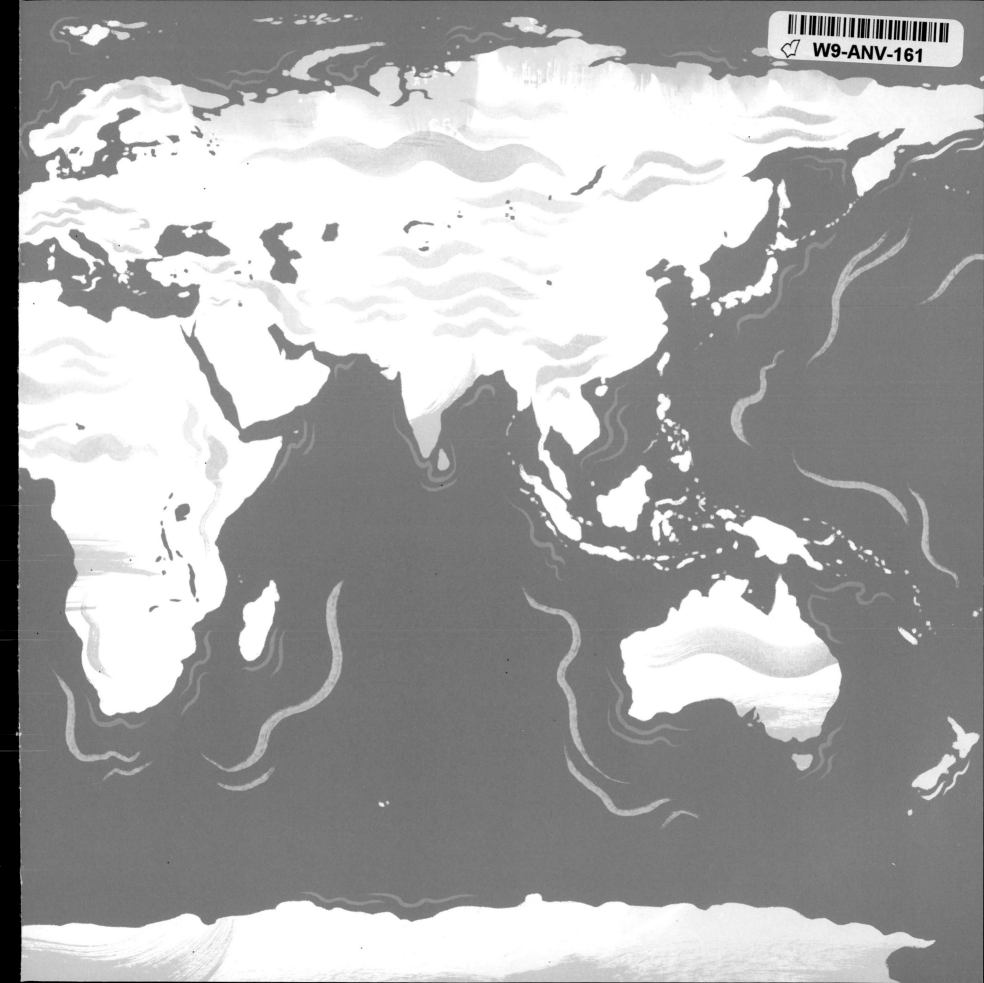

SECRETS OF OUR EARTH

Carron Brown

Illustrated by Wesley Robins

Kane Miller
A DIVISION OF EDC PUBLISHING

Earth is the world
where we live.

Journey to polar lands, dive
beneath the ocean waves and explore
rain forests and deserts to see the
wonders of our beautiful planet.

Shine a flashlight behind the page or
hold it up to the light to reveal what
is hidden in and around each landscape.
Discover a world of amazing surprises.

What is this hot, fiery ball in space?

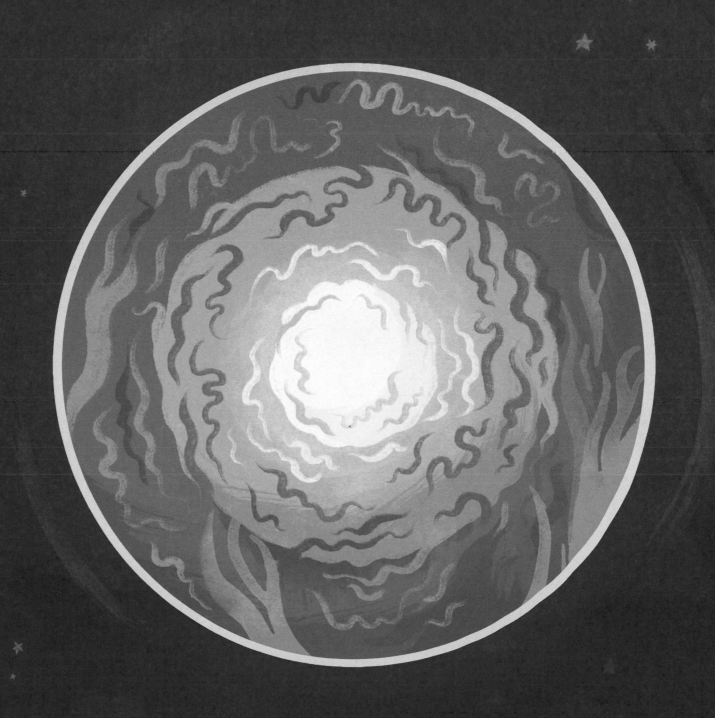

Is it the Sun?

No, it's the inside of Earth!

The inside is hot, but we live on the outside, which is cooler.

The sun is a star that gives Earth heat and light. It rises in the sky at dawn.

Can you see the whole sun?

The higher the sun climbs in the sky,
the brighter it gets, as night turns to day.

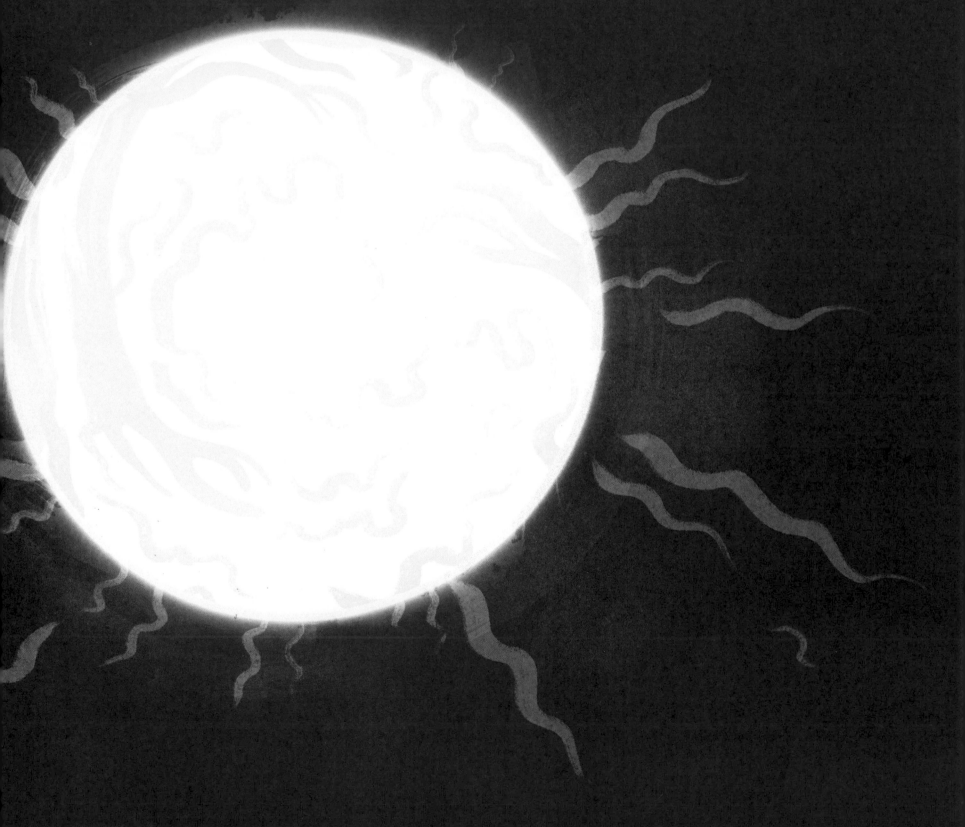

Mountains are the highest places on Earth. It is cold this far up, and it often snows.

Can you see a really big mountain?

Here it is!

A group of hikers is climbing the mountain.
They need to be careful—it's very steep.

Crunch!

Crunch!

Volcanoes are mountains that blow their tops.

What is shooting out of the volcano?

It's lava!

Lava is hot, melted rock from inside Earth.

It surges up through tunnels inside the volcano.

Whoosh!

Rivers flow from the land to the sea.
Water in rivers comes from rain and snow.

What's making a splash behind the cliff?

It's a waterfall.

River water falls
down a cliff into
the ocean below.

Roar!

All animals and plants need water to live.
Most of Earth's water is in the salty oceans.

Which animals live below the waves?

Many animals, both tiny and huge,
live in the oceans.

There are fish, turtles, dolphins,
corals, crabs and many more.

It is very cold and icy at the far north and South of Earth. Huge icebergs float in the Southern Ocean.

Can you See the whole iceberg?

There's much more ice below the surface of the water.

Penguins catch fish, and whales eat tiny creatures called krill.

The seashore is where the sea meets the land.
You can find rocks
and sand here.

Can you see the sand?

This beach is made of sand.

Sand is made of tiny bits of rocks and minerals that wash up on the shore.

Deserts are the driest places on Earth.
It hardly ever rains. Many sandy deserts
are very hot during the day.

Where do some animals go to keep cool?

It is cooler under the sand.

These jerboas live in tunnels underground.
They come out at night when it is cold.

Dig!

Dig!

Grasslands are large, flat areas where few trees grow.

Elephants eat grasses, which they pull up with their long trunks.

Who is watching them?

A group of meerkats is keeping watch.

They look out for danger and call
to each other if they spot trouble.

Peekaboo!

Rain forests are wet all year round.
Lots of plants grow in them.

We eat many rain forest fruits,
such as bananas and pineapples.

Who else eats the fruit?

Munch!

Spider monkeys climb up high
to eat fruit from trees.

Thousands of different types
of animals live in
rain forests.

Crunch!

It is stormy. The gray clouds are
full of raindrops, and lots of rain falls.

What kind of storm is this?

Rumble!

Crack!

It's a thunder and lightning storm.

Lightning is a bolt of electricity in the sky. After the lightning flash, there is a rumble of thunder.

Wind is air moving around Earth.

It can be a gentle breeze or a mighty gale.

What machines turn in the wind?

The blades of wind turbines are turned by wind to make electricity.

People live all around the world,
mostly in towns and cities.

Big cities are busy and crowded.

How many people can
you see on this train?

Night is falling. The sky turns red, and the clouds turn purple as the sun sets.

What can you see behind the clouds?

The moon and stars are up in space.

Shooting stars are pieces of space rock.
They burn up as they travel toward Earth.

A new day begins on this side of the world as night falls on the other side.

Wonderful things happen all around Earth every second of every day. What surprises will tomorrow bring?

There's more...

Climb mountains, swing through rain forests, trek over deserts and sail the oceans to find out more about Earth.

Mountain The highest mountain in the world is Mount Everest in the Himalayas. It is 29,029 feet tall.

Rain forest Rain forests grow where it is hot and rains a lot. The largest rain forest is the Amazon rain forest in South America.

Grassland Grasslands are called prairies in North America, pampas in South America, savannahs in Africa and steppes in Europe and Asia.

Polar lands The icy northernmost and southernmost parts of Earth are called polar lands. The North Pole is in the Arctic, and the South Pole is in the Antarctic.

Desert There are sandy deserts, rocky deserts and even icy deserts. Antarctica, an icy land, is Earth's largest desert. It's too cold for rain at the South Pole!

Ocean Earth has five oceans. From the largest to the smallest, they are the Pacific Ocean, the Atlantic Ocean, the Indian Ocean, the Southern Ocean and the Arctic Ocean.

River A river starts high up in hills or mountains, and most flow down to the ocean. Earth's longest river is the River Nile in Africa.

City A city has many buildings and is home to a lot of people. The largest city in the world is Tokyo, in Japan, where almost 38 million people live.

First American Edition 2017
Kane Miller, A Division of EDC Publishing

Copyright © 2017 Ivy Kids (an imprint of Ivy Press Ltd)

Published by arrangement with Ivy Press Limited, United Kingdom.

For information contact:
Kane Miller, A Division of EDC Publishing
PO Box 470663
Tulsa, OK 74147-0663
www.kanemiller.com
www.edcpub.com
www.usbornebooksandmore.com

Library of Congress Control Number: 2016934242

Printed in China

ISBN: 978-1-61067-536-9

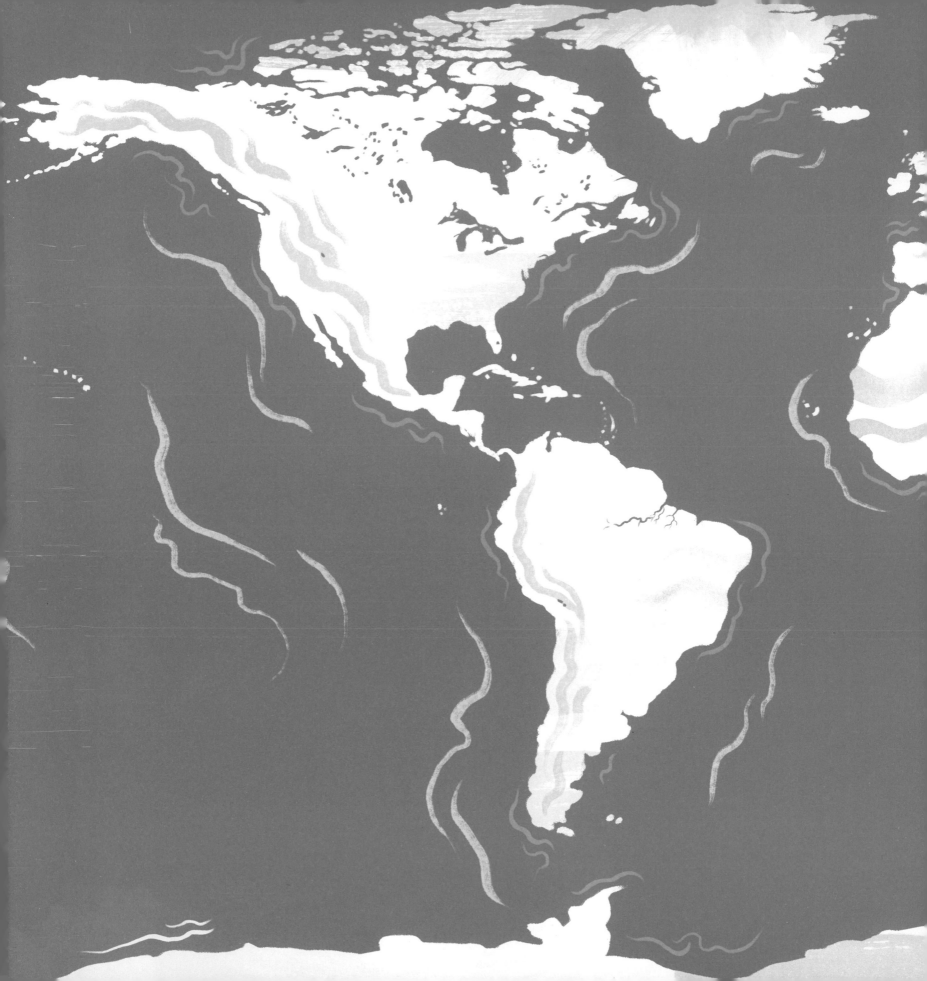